Nuru Life Poems

Forever grateful to Jesus Christ, our Lord and Saviour for salvation, the gift of righteousness and life in Christ.

The heavens are thine, the earth also is thine: as for the world and the fullness thereof, thou hast founded them. (Psalm 89:11)

Note from the editor

In this collection of poems, the reader will find poems that draw from God's word, His many blessings and experiences of His goodness from believers living life in Christ. We have enjoyed writing them and hope you will enjoy reading. The poems are suitable for the whole family. May the grace of our Lord Jesus Christ, and the love of God and the fellowship of the Holy Spirit be with you.

Table of Contents

Section one

Poems by Lilian Victoria Ogutu

Lilian is a disciple of Jesus Christ and has been writing for several years. She has two published books with children's short stories, Hadithi Fundi 1 and 2. Having grown up as a beloved daughter of a mother who served Christ in the Anglican church, and as part of a Christian family, she was baptized and confirmed in the faith. She has a pedagogical background, loves the Lord Jesus and by His grace continues in the Christian faith.

Searching for God

When searching for God,
There's no need to look far,
He's not in the clouds,
Or some far away star.

He doesn't hide in the shadows,
Even though He is hard to see,
"Obongo Nyakalaga" resides in the Spirit,
He's salvation and righteousness for us who believe.

In Christ our bodies are His temple,
So be good in the eyes of your Creator,
Receive grace to be faithful and honest,
And to Praise God everyday.

Believe God is in your spirit,
God is in your saved soul,
God is in your blessed heart,
God is love, this I believe and know.

Day by day

Day by day God walks with me,
And my burdens He helps me bear,
Each step I take along the way,
My loving Father is always there.

Day by day I believe God's love,
His love encircles me all around,
His grace and mercy cover me,
And raise me up when I am down.

Day by day the good Lord keeps me,
His angels encamp around me to protect,
Keep safe from the snare of the enemy,
Helps me please Him until Jesus returns.

Day by day I rely on my Heavenly Father,
To strengthen me with His word and Spirit,
He comforts with His wonderful love,
And to my heart He speaks godly peace.

Day by day God's presence guides,
Refreshes my spirit through fellowship,
God is faithful to watch over me,
More than a natural father watches over his children.

God's love

I believed and felt God's love today,
For the first time since I went stray,
I had felt guilt and shame for many years,
But God delivered me from those when I cried to Him.

By His grace I cried to Him and confessed my sin,
He opened the door and He let me in,
The good Lord greeted me with a smile,
Held me in His arms and said its been a while.

He assured me that its going to be alright,
Said that all that time I was filled with fear,
It was Him that protected and pulled me through,
For He had always been present.

He said He loved me since the beginning of forever,
And His pure love for me would never stop,
As His children we should know He's always present,
By faith we can choose to fellowship with Him in
prayer.

Good God

When" Nyasaye" created you,
He knew that He would see,
Someone that could choose,
What was good but also sometimes not.

Good God put you here on earth,
To live this blessed life you live,
Learning as you continue in it,
Giving the good you can give.

He knew that you would call on Jesus,
His beloved Son who loves,
When you stumble and need help,
Or choose foolishness and need His wisdom.

Good God had a good plan for you,
From the very beginning of creation,
With faith, love and hope,
He will give this plan to you.

Never doubt loving good God,
He knows you better than you know you,
Keep doing good as He leads you,
He sees the good you sow and will reward.

He will carry you if He needs to,
And hold you in His loving hands when in prayer,
He knows the plans and desires you have,
Each and every day.

What brought you to tears?
Someone gave up on you?
Look up to the good God who Created you,
Let all your faith be in Him alone.

I pray you see the light,
What I have been telling you,
The love that good God has for you,
Is infinite and greater than all the oceans.

Trust

I trust you good Lord,
I believe You know I do,
My inner thoughts you know,
Hold me close when I feel lost
Your love means everything to me.

Lord give me the measure of faith to know,
That every trial I go through in life,
You have been there and overcame,
For your word says you overcame the world.

I will rejoice in your finished work,
Rest by faith in what you have said,
Written as word and Spirit in the Bible,
Yes Lord you are forever good and merciful!

Section two

Poems by Margaret Akinyi

Margaret Akinyi is a born again believing Christian who loves Jesus Christ as personal Lord and Savior. She writes Christian poems to inspire people and exalt Jesus Christ. Margaret trained in National youth service and gained paramilitary, physical and mental skills to serve her Kenyan country and its people. She has also engaged in helping needy people through providing food, shelter, clothing and other basic needs. Currently she is involved in serving Jesus Christ in a local church.

Applied

Lord Jesus I take your holy blood and anoint my self,
the blood to forever shield and protect me,
the blood that cleanses all stubborn guilt stains,
the blood of Jesus like the scent of rose flowers,
the blood the protection instrument of pure love.

The blood of Jesus that quenches all thirst,
the blood of Jesus that shields from arrows of the devil,
the blood that protects the anointed one,
so evil arrows melt like wax melts before the fire,
the wicked disappear before the blood of Jesus.

The blood of Jesus is the peace covenant to mankind,
the blood that washes away mankind's sins,
this weapon of war, the armor of God,
the everlasting covenant, the deliverance from bondage,
the blood of Jesus is our everlasting covenant portion.

Purification

Precious Blood of Jesus purify us from all forms of defilement and pollution,
Precious Blood of Jesus purify both the living and the non-binding things,
Precious Blood of Jesus purify the houses, offices, land, and all that belongs to us.
Precious Blood of Jesus purify us from all forms of defilement and pollution.

Precious Blood of Jesus purify our, spirit, soul and body
Precious Blood of Jesus purify our minds of impure thoughts and evil imaginations.
Precious Blood of Jesus bail us from every arrest of sin and detention.
Precious Blood of Jesus purify us from all forms of defilement and pollution.

Precious Blood of Jesus cleans us from all forms of sinful desires,
Precious Blood of Jesus wipe away every writing and accusations of the enemy,
Precious Blood of Jesus purges our atmospheres of any demonic presence,
Precious Blood of Jesus destroy satanic challenges anytime, any day.

The power

The Blood of Jesus is the unique, effective and
powerful weapon for our deliverance.
The Blood of Jesus has never failed to produce the
expected victory by faith.

In Egypt many signs and wonders were done,
but Israelites were still under slavery of the Egyptians.
When the Blood of the Lamb appeared on the scene,
430yrs of captivity was broken and their slavery was
paid in full.

The Blood of Jesus is our mediator,
it is His life that bought us back to God from bondage.
The Blood of Jesus is our blessing, honor, and glory,
it takes away all that causes shame in our lives.

The Blood of Jesus is our advocate,
pleading Passover with God on our behalf.
The Blood of Jesus speaks better things than Abel's,
it does this on behalf of God's children by faith in Him.

Section three

Poems by Neema Penuel

Neema Penuel is a disciple of Jesus Christ. She loves the Lord and is a published writer of more than 150 poems. Her poems like" You Know Me," are published in a book collection of poems called" Words of Power" alongside 287 other poems. She is also active in mission work. This is by praying for the salvation of more people's souls and preaching the gospel of Jesus Christ, so Christ's truth and righteousness is known to many more. She is married to Jan, who is also a believer in Christ Jesus and together they are parents.

Grateful

Lord I am grateful for this,
i looked through the window,
and whoa what a sight,
saw snow falling softly.

Admired the pure white flakes,
that had traveled millions and millions of miles,
to reach earth just in times for this,
quiet moment of reflection where I sat.

My cup of hot coffee steaming,
warming me and reminding how cozy,
it is to be in a warm house,
there were others out there who did not have this.

They must endure the cold in unheated shelters,
Lord, good provider and Father of mercy,
i pray give me always abundance of what to give,
so others may also be well sheltered like I am.

In You

I saw a bird tweeting atop a branch,
its light weight balanced at the tip,
of one of the tiniest twigs
that grew on the green in my yard.

How did that little brown bird,
orange chested and gray winged,
know where to land and find stability,
if not its Cleaver Creator had inbuilt such knowledge.

For that I praise you living Lord God
your infinite wisdom is beyond our humanly wisdom,
causing this one to marvel and be mesmerized,
in you we all live, move and have our being.

Thank God

Thank God that's the Sun shinning,
its been so cold that words spoken seemed to freeze,
and water instantly turned to ice crystals,
on contact with that metallic door knob,
so the knob seemed smeared with corn floor.

The Sun is warm and kind today,
shinning brightly like the giant front lights of a car,
yet gentle to eyes like a flickering candle light,
that shone in those nights when electricity was a luxury,
and examination studies often done with lit candles,
but thank God that by His grace we made it so far.

Thank God for help to continue in the same grace,
and gratitude to know more and more of it,
some of us read for exams under the street lights,
candle lights," Nyangili" lamps and any resource,
that could give this treasure called light.

Cleansing

Thank you for cleansing me,
with the precious blood of Jesus,
that washes away red crimson sin,
resulting to beautiful white as snow,
Oh Lord, I am so refreshed!

Oh the blood of Jesus Christ,
has made me whole again,
washed away my every sin,
drawn me near to my precious Lord again,
like a hungry babe clings to its mother.

This precious blood is not just liquid,
but as the life of the animal is in the blood,
it is the life of Jesus Himself speaking therein,
cleansing like only God can do,
glory to God for this precious testimony!

How Timely!

To the little bird feeding on those berries,
i am amazed at how you got to that feed,
You are hungry I can see little one,
eat as much as you want,
for it is a timely provision,
for such a time as this,
when snow flakes are falling everywhere,
and your normal provision is frozen.

Yes, a timely provision,
just for you and your light feathery kind,
berries on a branch which my beloved,
pitted in the yard in earth and did not know,
that it will be a timely meal for you,
in the midst of this snow covered and frozen landscape,
a sign of heaven providing your meal,
Oh how timely indeed!

Light burden

I believe yours is a light burden dear Lord,
unlike that which weighed me down,
like a caravan donkey overloaded with baggage,
from things past, present and even future.

Now in this rest I say thank you good Lord,
only in you could I dare be at ease,
when circumstances seem to speak otherwise,
oh this Light that always displaces darkness.

I believe you are my Light gracious Lord,
which any created being can never switch off,
like a city on a hill that cannot be hidden,
your light shines brightly in my spirit being.

Look

Look at the stars,
He said to dear Abraham,
to see he had to look where He looked,
the stars spoke His language,
of things that were possible with Him,
in contrast to the human limitations,
in dear Abraham's mind.

Abraham believed Him,
he looked as He had instructed and saw,
believed and it was counted to Him for righteousness,
and whoa! The result He Almighty made manifest,
fruits of righteousness as many as the stars,
children of God who came through Abraham's faith,
therein are you and me who believed in Jesus Christ.

Expect Him

Hallelujah, He is coming soon,
even as we by faith wait now,
praying and keeping watch,
we know neither day nor hour,
except that His return is most welcome,
and His prosperous kingdom will be established,
on earth as in heaven, Amen.

Look well, the signs are there,
like the clouds signal when it will rain,
the Spirit, the water and His pure blood agree,
that the redeemeds' wait is not in vain,
Shalom be our portion as we expect,
to meet Him with fullness of joy,
like a beloved bride looks forward to meet her groom.

Seasons

Thanks be to God now and forever,
that the season for springing flowers is here,
see that budded apple tree in the yard,
telling the signs.

Lord thanks that you allowed me to see,
last month when it was still winter,
when snow rested atop the leaves,
of the leafless apple branches.

Again thanks be to God,
for the faith to see the summer,
when red ripe apples will fill the branches,
ready for others and the apple cake baker to pick.

God knows

Where there goes two fawns,
following each other like siblings,
wide eyed and seemingly innocent,
ignorant of who is watching their move.

Is that not something to marvel at,
a work of creation so simple,
yet so complicated again,
that only God knows it all.

The grass is greener on the other side,
it seems that's why they go there,
but looking at where they came from,
the grass might seem even greener.

Truly only God knows all answers,
to why they go here and there and thither,
their course of action like divinely guided,
He invites us to inquire from Him if we will.

God in nature

The" Nyangile" lamp once out,
see how light stars will be clear,
through the uncurtained window frame,
be free to look and marvel at God's creativity.
.
The dove once it flies away,
swaying in the evening sun,
the leafless hardy tree,
be inspired to look and reflect on His seasons.

The wild, yellow, plum fruits once ripe,
freely inviting to take and enjoy,
the good things given in nature,
think about these free delicacies that God made.

Believe

I believe that life is here,
now by faith in Him our dear,
the good Lord in whom salvation is sincere,
Who has given you righteousness and His word to hear.

I believe that as you hear and hear,
His word given so freely and near,
in your heart and in your mouth with no fear,
faith comes and grace to persevere.

I believe that as you persevere,
like a farmer sows seed during the year,
and patience helps him steer,
his expectation until harvest is clear.

I believe that there comes a joy of harvest,
after the season you spent in perseverance,
waiting patiently as the seeds grow and mature,
believe with me for the good from above.

The Way

Thank you Jesus for being the only way,
to the Father who loves us,
thank you for showing your humanity,
so all know to access this glorious truth,
and find salvation and righteousness that we all need.

Saul on the way to Damascus,
with his companions who knew no better,
thought he knew the righteous way for all,
so he persecuted the saved who believed in you,
he threw them into jail like those condemned.

You good Lord stopped dear Saul midway,
and you let him know it was You he persecuted,
blind and repentant he knew you as the way,
he got saved by calling on you as Lord,
and you revealed yourself to Paul as His righteousness.

More grace

The silence broken by a sound,
it's a Bible falling to the wooden floor, plop!
from the hands of the sitting reader asleep,
exhausted from the previous hours of diligent working,
the spirit willing but the body needs your strength,
more grace to be awake, read, meditate needed there,
gracious Lord, thank you for more of your good grace.

A similar event at Gethsemane,
Jesus disciples found sleeping in the garden, Zzz!
instead of watching and praying with Him for an hour,
the spirit willing His will, but the body doing its thing,
for in watching and praying there is overcoming,
more grace to watch and pray needed there,
gracious Lord, thank you for more of your good grace.

Amazing

A bare leafless tree sways silently,
small lively birds land on the branches,
twee, twee, twee, the tree comes alive,
the detailed wonders of beautiful creation manifested,
good God you never cease to amaze!

Beneath the tree are dry twigs and undergrowth,
nothing visible there in terms of food for humans,
yet the small birds know where their provision is,
they land to the ground in faith and begin feeding,
amazing that there is enough for every tiny beak.

They sow not, reap nor gather into barns,
yet our Heavenly Father feeds them to their content,
amazing, who did the sowing such that they found it?
perhaps a farm tractor I saw driving by last summer,
inadvertently, he served generous portions of" fresh"
wheat.

Content

Did you see the moon in the dark sky,
content to shine where placed to shine,
as dark clouds passed across its surface,
blown by the wind as if it were a chimney,
puffing dark smoke across its face.

Beloved of God, believer, know this,
seasons might come and go,
like the dark smoke that crossed the moon's surface,
yet did not change the core of the moon,
a core that God made perfectly stable.

Perfectly stable in Christ,
salvation in His name makes the believer's spirit,
and righteousness together with salvation,
in the inner person reborn in the image of good God,
more beautiful than the content moon's shine.

One thing

In the midst of a busy everyday,
a world where we always have one thing more,
to do in order to feel like we are in control,
i want this good part, the one thing that Mary chose.

You Lord Jesus confirmed that she had done so,
like a wise godly woman whom you had taught,
to be in your presence Lord,
sitting at your feet to hear your word.

Praying in understanding and tongues without ceasing,
overflowing with thanks to you Lord
for the abundance of good things I seek and find,
in your Holy word which is praiseworthy.

Grace to keep your word in my heart
through meditation like a sheep that ruminates,
drawing every good thing from it for prosperous use,
good Lord help me always choose your word.

Believe

Where is your faith?
sister have faith in God,
by it the just shall live He said,
vital like the fresh air we breath,
faith in God is faith in life now and forever.

Whom do you believe?
Brother be encouraged to boldly believe God,
in believing Him all things good are possible,
He said to fear not and only believe,
believing God is life now and forever.

Childhood

When I was a child,
the adults mentioned that Jesus is coming soon,
happily I received the message,
dreaming of all the play time I will have,
Kati, Mbara, Doli and more play.

I cherished the dream of no school but play,
then I was told to prepare for school,
and that dream sadly faded into disappointment,
not that I hated school and books,
play seemed the more attractive option.

Now I am grateful,
that somebody made me go to school,,
imagine if the child was left to its dreams,
playing all day long as it waits for Him,
not once did I contemplate the future.

Thank God for freedom to play,
and glory to God that Christ is surely coming soon,
yet the just shall live by faith now,
even as we look forward to His glorious coming,
when Christ establishes His glorious Kingdom on earth.

Lord God

Lord God thank you for being good,
your goodness keeps me believing your written word,
the Word agrees with your Spirit giving faith in you,
for without faith in you it is impossible to please you.

Lord God thank you for being perfect Love,
for without you it is impossible to have faith,
Your love and word casts out undesired fear,
and replaces it with perfect love, faith and hope.

Lord God thank you for being Holy,
your goodness keeps me in your holiness,
i live now by faith in your salvation and righteousness,
and in hope looking forward to Christ's glorious return.

Forgiven

Forgiven and freed from condemnation,
forgiven and redeemed from the curse,
forgiven and accepted in the beloved,
forgiven and restored to fellowship with Him,
in precious Christ we found forgiveness.

Forgiven you are through His precious blood,
forgiven through your faith in Him alone,
forgiven you are blessedly enabled to forgive others,
forgiven you are now free to live for Him,
in precious Christ you found forgiveness.

Forgiven with a pure forgiveness,
forgiven like Zachaeus the tax collector,
forgiven his hard heart was softened,
forgiven he was made free to be a good giver,
in precious Christ he found forgiveness.

Surround

Lord surround me with godly words,
that bring timely deliverance from destruction,
and nourish my soul with pure faith in You,
for this kind of faith pleases you good Lord,
like faithful Abraham who had faith in you.

Lord surround me with godly instructors,
who teach me to walk away from ungodly open doors,
and encourage to look to your loving care in Christ,
so this whole Christian life be a fellowship testimony,
like faithful Paul who was like a branch in the vine.

Lord surround me with godly brethren,
whose good faith examples stir your holy nature in me,
as a sanctified vessel fit for your purpose on earth,
preaching your gospel in season and out of season,
like faithful Christ preached this wonderful gospel.

Faith and conscience

Faith in God and a good conscience now,
are two friends that accompany the believer,
like the shadow that accompanies a man,
these two are your good companions.

Faith in God and a good conscience now,
are two virtues that cloth the royal in Christ,
like the valuable robe that covers a king,
these two bring great spiritual rewards.

Faith in God and a good conscience now,
are valuables that Jesus blood gave the believer,
like a man who gives an inheritance to his children,
these two keep your faith from being shipwrecked.

Faith and praise

Good Lord to our faith we add your praise,
as we seek your glorious, gracious face,
thank you for giving us the gift of peace,
timely salvation in your steadfast love and grace
for all who have believed in Jesus Christ as Lord.

Thanks that believers in you no longer have to guess,
that you are near us with your presence,
be magnified in our lives you who are most glorious,
as we call upon you who wills to raise,
our souls from the low place of desperate days,
where darkness like a curtain filters the Sun's rays.

In your loving presence darkness fades,
and in faith in you we experience your ways,
that are much higher and better than our ways,
as high as heaven is from earth He says,
may we dwell on your thoughts that are most glorious!

Coming Soon

Rejoice believer for Jesus is coming soon,
think about it when you see the sun,
that will be turned into darkness,
and the moon that will be turned red,
before the great and glorious day of the Lord,
and salvation for whoever calls on His name.
Oh rejoice with me for our Lord is coming soon!

Rejoice believer for the Lord's day is near,
let's put away the fleshly and invite his pure presence,
and our righteousness like a holy garment wear,
through faith in Him who saw our lives dear,
thereby through His cleansing blood drew us near,
and by His word gave us the new life that is perfect.
Oh praise Him with me for our Lord is coming soon!

Belong

Great all who belong to Jesus Christ,
apostle Paul wrote to the church in Philippians,
such a powerful word and meaning in" belong,"
like one being a property of another.

Yes, there are those who belong to Him,
not by power or might have they earned this place,
not by the good works presented before Him,
but by faith in Him who by His blood bought them.

Friend I ask now whether you belong to Him?
by faith I believe and know that I belong to Him.
gracious Jesus Christ, my Saviour and Lord,
who bought me with His precious blood.

Only

Only when the blood of the lamb had cleansed,
could the Holy Spirit indwell,
in the cleansed vessel by faith,
this means faith in God who did the cleansing.

Without the cleansing of the lamb's blood,
our works though good in the eyes of fellow mankind,
and in our eyes, cannot be good enough,
to make fit for the Lord's indwelling.

Only through the cleansing of the blood,
have we passed from death to eternal life,
this life is more precious than a million tonnes of gold,
and now we live to please Him and hope in His return.

Life

Lord thank you for your precious blood,
where your life speaks every good thing,
in the life of the christian believer,
like the blood of a lamb spoke Passover to evil,
and the blessing of protection to the Israelites.

On that precious Passover night in Egypt,
the life that is in the lamb's blood,
spoke better things than the blood of Abel,
every one who had taken refuge in a marked dwelling,
whose doorposts showed the mark was protected from
the destroyer.

Lord Jesus you have deemed our lives valuable,
in deed so much that you willingly gave yours,
so we who did not deserve it could live,
may my heart overflow with gratitude,
on recalling your blood that saved and made me
righteous.

Joy

Good Lord your joy is my strength,
when I think of what you have said,
take you at your word as God,
build the word into my inner being,
joy, joy, joy unspeakable results.

Your word is my light,
sealed for perfection with the lamb's blood,
that precious Jesus shed in the cross,
so the sins of the world be wholly forgiven,
and I was part of the world, but now a child of God.

Yes, I believe I am born again and saved,
translated from the kingdom of darkness,
where the man of sin reigned as god,
into that powerful kingdom of light,
where Jesus is King of kings and Lord, Hallelujah!

Infinite Value

Lord God and Jesus thank you,
for giving what was of infinite value,
even 120,000 sheep and 22,000 oxen,
combined could not measure up in value,
to the blood of the sin free Lamb.

Thank you for paying to buy me,
from the shelf of sin's shop,
where the sin of Adam had sold me,
from the very beginning when he disbelieved,
God's word and instead believed the lie.

Now I believe and know,
whom I belong to forever,
Him who spared not His best,
but freely gave for my deliverance,
hallelujah to the Righteous Lord God who saves.

Encouragement

In Christ we can encourage the weak,
His Word instructs let the weak to say" I am strong,"
oh, how glorious is this truth, Hallelujah!

He took our weaknesses and instead,
gave us His divine strength,
through the blood of the lamb, so precious!

I was weak but now by faith made strong in Him,
you dear sister were also weak then,
now you have been made strong in Him; only believe!

That is why I can encourage you,
that in Him you can do all things,
through Christ who strengthens you, blessed forever!

Laugh

God who sits in heaven laughs,
not at his children but at his defeated enemy,
for when the blood of the lamb was shed,
God's best was given to eternally seal,
the defeat of him who went about the earth,
seeking whom to deceive into sin and devour,
haha, haha, haha!

After this sacrifice of the lamb,
the righteous Son Jesus whom God offered,
for sins of mankind from yesterday, today and forever,
Jesus entered rest knowing full well,
that enemy was forever defeated,
made his footstool once and for all,
now by faith we labour to enter His rest,
Hallelujah, Hallelujah, Hallelujah!

Go ahead laugh for joy with loving God,
through the lamb's blood He gave us the victory,
in Christ Jesus gave us authority in His name,
to go into the whole world and preach His gospel,
in the power of the Spirit who He gave us at salvation,
with expectation that all attached to the enemy,
are under His feet and now under believers feet too!
Glory, glory, glory to God!

Only because

Only because of your precious blood Lord Jesus,
Can we come boldly before the throne of grace,
prophesying in thanksgiving and praise to exalt You,
like Heman the King's seer and his 14 promise sons,
who ministered in God's great house under King David,
thank You lord for Your given precious life
hallelujah; for its Your godly life in the blood..

Only because of this precious blood of the lamb,
can we believe that we are vessels of gold,
in You, God's great house, sanctified for Your use,
ready for every good work as You will,
for to please You now as we expect Christ's return,
is a privilege of the saved who have believed in You.

Only because of the blood of Jesus plead upon us,
who have believed You as Lord and Saviour forever,
by faith that you God died, was buried and resurrected,
are we continually cleansed from every sin,
that tries to cling and weigh down the believers,
so that we cannot run the race set before us with ease,
but You gives the grace to walk in the light.

Testimonies

Thank you Lord for testimonies,
our heritage in Christ, the Bible says,
forever witnessing of your word,
and the blood of the precious Lamb,
as weapons that overcame the devil. Hallelujah!

With marvel I read the testimony,
of early Christians who have been saved,
and made righteous in you, Jesus our Lord,
desired to be filled with your Holy Spirit and prayed,
You gave but Satan hindered the manifestation. Oh!

Instead of giving up and focusing on sin,
they were instructed to focus on Christ's righteousness,
plead the lamb's blood that made them righteous,
as they plead in faith and expectation of your answer,
testimonies manifested in speaking in tongues!

Preserved

I love you Lord now and forever,
through your precious blood shed on the cross,
you made me peculiar and now I belong,
to your body as a blessed member,
and your pure love and word preserves me
so that my life my be to your glory,
living by faith to please you now in hope of your return.

Holy, holy, holy are you Lord,
heaven and earth are full of your glory,
as the redeemed, you have enabled me by grace,
to worship you in spirit and in truth,
together with the blood washed saints,
whom by faith in God you preserve
until your second coming oh glorious Lord.

Free indeed

LORD Jesus thank you for this freedom,
innocence that makes me bold in your presence,
knowing that in Christ there is now no condemnation,
to those who by faith walk after the Holy Spirit,
believing in the cleansing power of the Lamb's blood.

LORD be glorified for this freedom,
not wrestled into by place by my power or might,
but by your Holy Spirit given me at salvation,
through faith in the finished work of the cross,
for this life forevermore thank you good Lord.

LORD thank you for this new covenant,
sealed with the blood of the Lamb,
in you Christ in whom is my freedom indeed,
and grace to live by faith in you,
who redeemed me and made me yours forever.

Use the weapon

A weapon is best for its use,
and the knowledge of how to use it,
coupled with faith in its ability.

The powerful precious blood of Jesus
and the word of God are the best weapon,
to establish the victory that Christ already won.

Establishing this victory is all by faith in Him,
that comes by hearing and hearing,
by the word of God, dear brethren.

The Israelites on Passover night,
had faith in Him who spoke the word,
to mark their doors with a lamb's blood.

Resting inside the lamb's blood marked houses,
by faith in Him who had spoken and His word,
their dear lives were preserved from the destroyer.

What a glorious testimony dear brethren,
speaking of what Jesus Christ did to preserve Israel,
and is doing now for believers in Him.

Living to please Him now by faith,
and by His grace expecting His second coming,
let us use this weapons of preservation faithfully.

The Holy Spirit

In the Old Testament in faith,
the priest first applied the blood of the lamb,
then the Holy Spirit could fill the cleansed,
glory to God for this testimony,
of the power in the blood of the Lamb,
and this was just a shadow of the things to come.

In the early church,
believers newly born again and desiring the overflow,
pleaded the blood of Jesus by faith,
sometimes repeatedly like water cups filling a pot,
when the overflow happened, thank God,
they began to speak in tongues as the Spirit led.

What is there in it for us today?
See Daniel prayed and God answered immediately,
but it took three weeks before the answer came,
for demonic forces fought God's angels meanwhile,
trying to stop the answer from reaching Daniel,
so he could lose faith in the God who answers prayers!

Now in the Spirit we can faithfully pray in Jesus name,
plead the blood of Jesus for immediate answers,
for it is a weapon of victory forever,
to which the demonic has no answer,
but they must give way to the victory already given,
when Jesus cried on the cross," It is finished."

He hates it

Lord Jesus thank you for your life in your blood,
you who loves righteousness and hates evil,
and whom God anointed with the oil of joy,
more than all your peers, Hallelujah!

LORD we know from your word and Spirit,
that the devil hates the life in the Lamb's blood,
and would rather we your children forget about it,
for it torments his very evil nature.

In obedience to your word,
we obey to plead your precious blood,
for only because it was shed were we forgiven,
made free to hate evil and love righteousness in You.

Lord Jesus thank you for your blood,
which the devil hates for it destroyed his works,
but we by faith plead, honor and joyfully sing about,
for in it is our salvation and righteousness. Glory!

Answers

What could wash away our sins?
What could save and make us righteous before God?
What could make us whole again?
Nothing but faith in the living blood of Jesus. Glory!

How could the Lamb's blood wash away our sins?
How could it save and make us righteous before God?
How could it make us whole again?
Not by power or might but by His Spirit. Glory!

Where do I find the Lamb's blood to wash my sins?
Where do I find it to save and make me righteous
before God?
Where do I find it to make me whole again?
In my Lord Jesus whose blood was shed on the cross at
Calvary. Glory!

Your tangible presence

Lord Jesus you are so wonderful,
you have given us your precious blood,
to take by faith and cleanse,
 every area of our spirit, soul,
manifesting in the body too,
Glory to God!

Now Lord thank you,
for what you are doing through faith in you,
as I take your precious blood and take a priestly wash,
from the top of my head to the soles of my feet,
in the morning as I awake and in the evening.
You are good and your mercy endures forever!

Your presence is tangible in your blood,
and when we as called royal priesthood to your glory,
by faith apply it for washing and cleansing,
confessing your forgiveness and healing,
in every life's area thru' the finished work on the cross.
Gracious God!

Lord thank you for when thoroughly clean
like fresh snow from heaven,
we believers like shinning light in a dark world,
can lead many more sinners to you for salvation,
and knowledge of your truth,
Hallelujah!

Printed and published by: BoD - Books on Demand, Norderstedt
ISBN: 9788743033592